# One Breath at a Time

A little girl remembers to breathe through
it all...

# K.D.Brown

**ROYSTON**
Publishing

BK Royston Publishing

P. O. Box 4321

Jeffersonville, IN 47131

502-802-5385

http://www.bkroystonpublishing.com

bkroystonpublishing@gmail.com

Cover Design: Gad, Ecover Elite


ISBN-13: 978-1-946111-70-8


Printed in the United States of America

# I Write This Book in Honor of My Mother
# Patricia Ella Dickson

For all the courage, strength, and love she always had.

May we find closure and peace as your legacy lives on forever...

This high school graduation photo which she so proudly distributed to one of her aunt's read...

"To the best aunt out of this world! You would have never believed that I made it, but Aunt Mickie, I did." 1966. Love Always, Pat.

As I look at this picture and read between the lines of "you would of never believe I made it," I can only think she was referring to so much more than completing high school.

# Dedication and Love to...

My Father Coleridge Dickson II,
Who always tried his best while dealing
with his own past.

My Brother Andrew "Mit" Dickson
Sr.,
For putting up with as much as he could,
for as long as he could.

My Twin Sister Kathy Dickson-
Crawford,
Who will always share my thoughts,
feelings, and pain,
She also holds a book deep within

My Older Sister Lorena "Lisa"
Dickson-Burton,
Who has lived, seen & been
I commend her for always holding her
head up high

My Husband Pastor Garry M. Brown
For having an abundance of patience and
tolerance while loving me with his all

# &

## My Children
### Daryl Poole Jr., Eddie Servance III, & Douglas Servance

For without my three special gifts, I would
have lost myself long ago.
You will never know the magnitude of love
I carry for you all

# Special Acknowledgements

Above all, I must acknowledge God the Father for without Him I would not be physically, emotionally, or mentally sound. During the darkest points of my life, when I thought I was forgotten, felt so broken, neglected, and abused, I now know He kept me. My Father, I love & praise you.

To my lovely Aunt Ernestine "Tina" Johnson who was placed in my life to serve as an auntie/mommy and does it with no hesitation. The love she pours into me is unexplainable, I am overwhelmed with gratitude and smiles just thinking about how much she means to me.

To all who the Lord has graciously allowed to cross my path, to be a spark of light for me when times may have been dark, I say many blessings to you all.

Most of you have been my rock when I felt I couldn't handle things any longer. Many of you have given me so much comfort, strength, guidance, and love when I didn't think I could bare another day. All of you have loved me unconditionally during the good and bad times. May you always remember, I know my life has been touched because our paths crossed.

# Author's Note

It is so very true that when you begin to confess your sins to the Lord, something makes you want to hesitate, when you want to shout of His great doings, something makes you hesitate, when you want to tell that testimony that you know will help millions, something makes you hesitate.

I will hesitate no more. I have confessions. I will shout of His great doings. I will stand proud to give my testimony. I will ignore the nightmares I am having that are resurfacing from my past, for I know it is only something trying to stall what I need to share. Satan can get thee behind. There will be no more hindrance of my soul.

I write this book not to belittle anyone who may have been a part of my life at one time or another but to keep myself uplifted while possibly uplifting another.

To all who the Lord guides to read this book, I pray that you take my words deep within. For if my story can touch, comfort, and start the healing process for one, then my mission has been met.

# Table of Contents

# Prologue

I have many happy memories of my childhood. Playing outside with my siblings and many cousins, being around lots of family members during the holidays or summer months. I remember laughter, smiles and fun. As I grew older and could start to place thoughts together that were tucked far away in my mind, I began to ask myself were they all good times? Or was I imagining or even dreaming up this wonderful life to cover up the hurt and pain that was suppressed so far within. I remember many years of thinking my life was a dream after I lost my mother. I learned years later that my siblings and I were present when she was murdered although absent from the funeral, as it was stated, "too much for us to handle." I still have no remembrance of this while growing up. My own belief is her last words to me as she looked down with the kindest eyes and softest voice and saying, "Stay here, I will be right back." To a child, you never want to give up hope that anyone will not come back. You keep that sentence so bottled up in your mind that you believe in your heart they will do as they said and come right back no matter how many years have passed. You are mentally at that time in your life when you last heard that precious voice. Having to learn how to differentiate what was happening in my life during specific time frames was very hard because a big part of me was still that little girl waiting on the sidewalk curb waiting for her mother to return.

# One

# Breath

# at a

# Time

## Chapter 1

I knew I couldn't be selfish with my testimony after two incidents stood still in my memory for some time. Once, a young lady who walked into my office one day with a look on her face that I had seen in my own mirror so many times. And second while sitting in the dentist office to look over at a child who payed close to a conversation I was having with another regarding writing a book. The child possibly in six or seventh grade calmly asked me what was my book about? As I began to tell her of it, to my surprise, she looked at me with a familiar look and response, "I have been through a lot too."

Wow I thought as I said to this young lady, "Honey no matter what, always know you can pull through anything. God has a mighty plan and will never be apart from us." I then told this precious child to keep holding her head up and stay as strong as I could see she was.

There are far too many of us out there who know the look, who feel the pain of the past or are still carrying worries of an unknown tomorrow. Therefore, we must pay attention, acknowledge, guide, love, and support even if only with a listening ear or a gentle smile. We must remember that when we talk, we must know that the person you least expect is listening, growing, and healing.

I write about my life and the trials and tribulations I have endured and how I came through them all at certain times in my life never realizing that while going through the pain, someone was always close protecting me.

It is truly amazing how you can go through issues as a child or young adult and you tend to block many instances out of your mind, so much to the point of having to remind yourself to breathe when forgotten and suppressed thoughts cross your mind. I remember once sitting and watching television and my mind wandered off to an unfamiliar place. Before I knew it, I was gasping for air. It's like my mind and train of thought just stopped.

I instantly thought a past memory was trying to push through into my current thoughts. I knew the memory would change my feelings at the time, make the past pain resurface, and clog my mind for a period. Could I withstand that on this day? Typically, I wouldn't want the unfamiliar thoughts to resurface due to remembrance hurting. I would say to myself, why must I go through it again? Did I not endure enough mentally, emotionally, and physically when that time in my life took place?

Currently I invite the memories as I am no longer scared of the unknown, of my shaky and unpredictable past. Having taught myself to deal with what I now know to be an anxiety attack and slowing down enough to breathe through a thought, I now invite all memories, so I can continue to grow within.

I sit day in and day out wondering when people are going to get it together within enough to turn all the hard times around while striving to make a change so the future can be so far from the past. Emotions build up within me as I think of the useless energy. We use to try and keep negative, hurtful situations, and painful thoughts going in our lives. I know too well that it may feel as if we cannot live or go on because of the situations happening in our lives today and more painfully yesterday. We must get to the point when we ask ourselves is the aggravation, strife, degradation, and just common disrespect worth it. You may feel like you are the only one going through your situation and like it will never end. Remember and be assured that there are many people wearing the same shoes and one day you will be able to breathe without having to remind yourself.

To those with minimal or no responsibilities, no children as of yet, no attachments who are in situations that are hindering your spirit, you are feeling belittled, disrespected and abused while feeling self-worth fading, I encourage you to take three steps back and pull yourself out of the picture. Looked into it and find the way to build you back up. Find a way to push yourself in a direction you thought was so far away. Repaint the picture with the brightest colors and most beautiful scenery you can imagine. At some point in my life, I allowed the picture in my mind to become the sight that allowed me to see and be past so much hurt.

One day I realized that everything in life for me was a test and training for today and my future that God needed me to experience. Having gone through what I felt to be more bad than good, in "this thing I call life," I can only believe it was what molded and shaped me while preparing me for what's next.

Will we ever understand it all? Surely some of it may make sense at times while

7

what we cannot handle today will enter our mists when we are ready mentally and emotionally to bare it.

Having to learn the hard way not to accept broken apologies and that friendships and true love should never hurt and surely not leave you messed up physically, emotionally and mentally while creeping into your spiritual mind set. Once we understand what self-respect, self-esteem, self-worth, and self means, we then can take a hold of our lives as we bloom and grow into so much more than we could ever fathom.

As time and internal growth took place, I soon learned self-respect and who I was. I learned to thank God for me and who

He created me to be no matter what my past had dictated. I had to dig deep after I knew I could and learned that I did have a relationship with God who I thought had left little ole me long ago. I then took a deep look into 2 Peter 3:9 "God is being patient with you. He does not want anyone to be lost, but He wants all people to change their hearts and lives".

I do not write these words to make one feel less of self or to push towards healing in any manner as everyone's time table is different in all capacities. I share as I know it is time while speaking from so deep within my soul. In doing so, I tear up and get the tightness within my stomach just thinking deeply about it all and what one little girl could endure, one young lady could withstand, and one broken soul could hold onto with little or no hope.

Having been through more than I wish to rethink, I now know it is time to stop being quiet as doing so would continue to keep me in bondage and the pain would continue to eat at me as I tried alone to make sense of it all. Therefore, I talk, talk, and talk more each day. Why? I share with hopes that one out of a million will lift their head up with a partial smile and know they are on the way to freedom from it all while knowing my mission has been met. When I extend a helping hand, it is because I have more than less traveled down the same dark road where the sign read Dead End for way too long. When I extend shelter, food, a listening ear, or shoulder to cry on, it is not to be high and mighty but simply because I know we all may end up in the same predicament one day, if we haven't already.

It truly hurts me to know that in this time we are still going through so much pain putting people through hurt and accepting it. Too many continue to watch and ignore the problems rather than dealing with them. Also, I cannot fathom why after all we have been through (people of all races and nationalities), we can't come together and stop hurting and belittling each other. To make matters worse, we also continue to do it to ourselves. Seriously, just pure ignorance.

I don't know everyone's situation and Lord knows I wish I could sit, listen, and be there for all who need and are ready to speak. Always know there are people who care and who will listen and assist. Don't pull back so far within that you are afraid to talk or seek help. Your opinions, thoughts, and words are oh so important. When you feel you cannot take that next step, like the road is about to end and no one cares, remember we serve and awesome God who has already placed the answers within us. We must listen deeply and not just hear what's going on around us but open our eyes to see and not just look. Then we can start to embrace, receive, and understand what is needed at that moment and start going in the right direction.

I share my own testimonies more than less at this point in my life as I relate so deeply with so many I come across day to day. I have learned to no longer accept excuses from myself or allow how I am feeling to hinder my growth no matter the situation. I've learned enough was stripped from me in my early life and I couldn't allow it to resurface. When I sit and think of what a younger me had to endure, I think about how that same little girl survived as the tears roll down my cheek and a slight breath is taken. I believe the most painful part of it all is that too many of us carry intentional and some unintentional pain inflicted by others without knowing because they were in fact dealing with their own hurt and pain or burying it and thinking they were moving on.

The best thing to do when we learn better, start to heal, and try to move forward on the positive side of the road is remember we will make some bad choices, make left turns instead of right at times and that we will not always make the right decisions and that's okay. "For a just man falleth seven times and riseth up again; and the wicked shall fall" Proverbs 24:16. No matter what, He will never leave us nor forsake us. That is enough assurance for me that we are not alone during the fights and struggles, even when we feel so alone and forgotten.

¹⁰*"Finally my brethren, be strong in the Lord and in the power of His might. ¹¹Put the whole armour of God that ye may be able to stand against the wiles of the devil. ¹²For we wrestle not against principalities, against powers, against the rulers of darkness of this world. Against spiritual wickedness in high places. ¹³Wherefore take unto you the whole armour of God, that ye may be able to withstand in the evil day and having done all, to stand".* Ephesians 6:10-13 (KJV)

Situations of the past will take time to get over and learn to live with. Although we may never forget and may go through instances that a trigger may arise causing the pain to resurface, we can learn to move forward with full force. We can learn to take the pain, hurt, and anguish and build on it. Push forward like we have never pushed before. Slowly we can learn how not to allow our spirit to be hindered with old worries because we cannot change them.

Sadly, as with all, I struggle with some hurt from the past. Once I remind self to breathe, I take the next step forward.

## Chapter 2

I sit and think of how different my life would have been if my mother wasn't taken from me when I was barely old enough to hold on to memories of a smile and knowing what her voice sounded like. Would I have endured so much trauma which started at such an early age and at the hands of the family, or would I have lived a life as many who state how a "normal life" is...

Not knowing all the details of how, when, and why my mother was murdered when I was 6 years old, caused a lot of internal pain and lost as I grew up in a world of unknown and at times making up what I thought made sense for the moment.

Wondering if what I heard some say was true or what others said was false made trust and disbelief play a big part in a lost child's mind.

A person disappeared from my life. When I sit and think about how I can only remember casual periodic conversations about her. I am sure not one person wanted to be the one to have the heart to heart conversation and possibly receive a question that would hurt them to answer. I grew up listening more than I spoke in many scenarios thinking a lot of what if and I wonder, wonder, wonder. I found strength in some telling me I carry my mother's kindness and want to assist and help all. Some tell how I protect and love my children and grandchildren in the same manner she did her very own children. I sit during Mother's Day weekend each year hurt, pained, in deep thought for a period. smile through it while embracing her grands and great grands knowing she would have with so much passion.

I grew up waiting to hear how my mother passed, was it an accident, shooting, WHAT?! only to learn during 1991 at the age of 22, with 2 small children, while sitting in the Stamford Connecticut Library's lower level. The library housed the microfilm. I began to look up the newspaper for the year 1975, month of August. It was the only concrete information I had at the time relating to any

19

facts. What I learned caused a young girl, whose mind was not ready to house such information, sitting in a place of no assurance, a quiet place where composure had to be kept, noise to the most minimal, shock had to be held within. As I scrolled through the microfilm, I reached the newspaper article with minimum information listed that read Stabbing Victim Dead. I kept my composure and began to print the article from the newspaper so I could share it with my siblings as well as use it to piece some more of my shattered life together. There is always a time in our life when we need the whys, who, and wheres answered by someone. We must stop shutting doors and dismissing what is needed to become known, because someone is hurting, suffering, and trying to make sense of it all.

The pain of my mother's loss did not end there. I continued to seek, learn, and know more about her. I sought out her father, after learning the man who's name she carried, was not her biological father and entered her life only to cause hurt, pain, and not treat her as a father should. To hear about some of what she endured and know my past causes so much pain and despair, I know, should she had been allowed to stay in my life, she would have been my shield through it all. She would have picked up on every sign, red flag, the sadness in my eyes, the hurt in my voice,

21

and the body language that was exhibited in so many ways.

Upon finding this man who was merely a donor and never a father, I learned he was always close in the neighborhood. Who knew he had a daughter and several grandchildren that he never supported, asked about or looked for? The saddest part is that I have some family members who are related to him in other ways through his family. I got up enough strength one day to place my children in the car and drive across town (with my aunts help as she knew where he was) to this man's place of business and introduce myself to him letting him meet his great grandchildren. The initial part of the conversation was short with no affection and he passed the children a dollar or two to get some candy or whatever (as many elders did back in the day). We parted shortly after. The awkwardness was a bit much for me. Several months later, I felt it in my heart to make a visit again. I wanted to see if I could learn more of his family, who else are we related to, etc. only to pull up and he ask me if I was coming around to get money from him. This man had no clue who he was speaking to as I never asked anyone for anything. After taking a deep breath, I reminded him that I have never expected anything from someone who couldn't find it in their heart to do anything for their own child. No matter what was going on in my life, I always took care of myself, and that he could rest assured that he would never have to worry about me or my children seeking him out anymore. Since that day in the early 90's, I have not seen him. I learned he passed away sometime later. What bothered me about his death was a family member stated someone provided his family with me and my sibling's information for his obituary. I haven't sought out the truth about this. I only can wish it is not true.

To go through so such and at certain moments, actually feel a closeness to my mother who was long gone still hurts.

The close feeling made me able to relate to so much hurt and pain that it makes my chest hurt while I try to understand it all.

Time and added hurt have no schedule in our lives.

Several years later, in 1994, we lost my dear brother who was only a year younger than my twin and I. This came as a shock being it was merely a year after losing a cousin who I was very close to. They were the same age and grew up together during their short lives. My brother, who carried just as much as me if not more, just couldn't take another step in this thing called life and one morning took his own life.

I will never forget the phone call, the yelling and the long wait for my husband at the time to reply to over 40 pager pages that I sent to him on that day. The distance I felt from life, the chest pains and having to remind myself to breathe still feel so fresh today. Will we ever know the concluding factor that makes someone move to the unknown, feel so distant and lost, while so many are left behind wondering daily what could have been done differently? While daily trying to push forward without continuing to ask ourselves what I could have done differently? After I learned how my brother had shot himself, I viewed his body at the mortuary. I can still see him lying on the table with his light skinned face, soft hair color with a straight hairline across his forehead, wearing white t-shirt and grey sweatpants with one pant leg pushed up to his knees (as he always wore them.) At that moment, I felt everything leave me from within. The finalization of it all had hit me. He was gone... telling myself to breathe as I had to do oh to many times in my life, I thought to myself he was finished with it all. He couldn't continue to pretend. No longer could he smile that beautiful smile. No longer would he have to remember our past, while trying to fight through the days to make it to an unknown future. I leaned over and kissed my baby brother's face for the very last time as I held his hand and told him it's okay. I know he needed to hear that.

Dealing with so much hurt and pain or when you try to deal with so much hurt and pain can take you to a different place within causing you to be very emotional or unemotional from time to time. I honestly can't explain the pain I endured when my brother died or the hurt, I still feel today.

## Chapter 3

After such a great loss I believe that is when my Grandma Johnson "Toots" felt it was time to share some information. She finally could see her babies (as she called us) were slipping away for lack of information, guidance, and truth. She could now see the pain and hurt while finally hearing our silent cries as we continued to misunderstand it all living in the shadows of trauma, continued abuse, and ignorance of it all. Because of this, we couldn't continue to smile and fake it day in and day out.

We had a family who some hugged, all smiled when gatherings occurred, and many times some joy was present although what was love? Who said I love you? Who said it's going to be okay? Who said one day it will make sense? Who said you are important? You will excel? Who, Who, Who? I asked this for many years as I tried to make sense of my life not anyone else's just mine. I had to remind myself of the age of those before me, the situations they have not healed from, and the hurt and pain they were still running from. The word trauma, which was not a word back in the day, and I began to make excuses. I continued to cover up, suppress, and push forward. After my grandmother talked my husband, at the time, into bringing me to her house to gather some of my mother's information so I could find some peace and closure, I hesitantly agreed to go. The fear of the unknown is scary and opening the truth hurts as we revisit a time that we never wished to be true.

As I sat in my grandmother's kitchen, which I so happily remember, she always had everything set up so orderly with nothing out of place. Her trinkets were in the same spot as you remembered from past visits. I began to ask myself am I ready for this, can I handle it, why am I the only one here? As grandma walked into the kitchen with a large brown envelope in her hand and a few books, she stated, "Karen I know it's time to give you this. I should have talked to you all years ago."

I believe my brothers passing prompted this and she was fearful to lose another if not physically but mentally as well.

She passed me the items and the first thing I read was a letter my father had written to my mother on March 15, 1975 at 10:35 pm. The letter basically states how the relationship was being dissolved and they had both previously spoke about it and agreed. He didn't want to cause any misery for others and since it was very hard to rap about it, the letter was written. I do not know how my mother perceived this letter, what her thoughts were, if she shared it with anyone, or just tucked away in a drawer. As I read it over and over, I paid close attention to the words that she underlined with a pencil <u>Long Time,</u> <u>Compatible, We, Think, I've, All, Ample</u>). By the darkness of it, she pressed hard making me wonder what she felt. What was she thinking? Did she have to remind herself to breathe at that very moment. After re-reading it I questioned, did she underline the words or did he...

As I finished reading the first letter, I went on to the next which was addressed to me and my three siblings. I assume it was written on or around the same period of March 1975. It was very brief and to the point as to why my father had to leave for a while and that he loved us all very much and to listen to Mommie...

The next letter I picked up was from my mother. She had it written to herself on the 31st of July 1975 which was a Thursday. She writes "Today I quit my job before 11:00 am. Came home to greet my man, F-A-S-T, Because He going to check out Boston! He wasn't Home, Bag all Pack! I waited on a call, but no Happens on my end of line, He no I don't have a Dime, so what's up, let me know something "Any-thing!""

I honestly do not remember reading all of what was in the envelope until I pulled the documents out recently to re-read as I wrote this book. I had to pause and sit very still as I tried to put together what she had been going through from March to July. What prompted her to write this note? How was she coping? Was she coping? Was my mother still smiling at us as she tucked us into bed at night whispering it will be all right only to go to her room and cry wondering was it really going to be all right. How was she coping at work prior and then dealing with four children with little to no means except whatever family support may have been given. What did she think? What does a 26-year-old think?!

I kept asking myself remembering myself in a similar situation with three children not to long ago, would I have made different choices and decisions if this little information was shared with me?

I grew up in a closed world that felt as if I looked or questioned if all the glass would break. Being scared to ask what and why for fear of making someone else feel less of and through it all worried about someone else's feelings. Because we all hear from everyone no matter where we come from, "I am trying my best."

Children don't understand that. We need more in all areas, we need some truth, more conversations more of it all. Because when we don't have it, we stay in that room that will shatter at any moment. Then before I moved on, I glanced back over at the papers in front of me, looked at the dates again, read very carefully what my mother had written, and immediately said aloud to myself, why did she quit her job? If she rushed home to her man (my father), when and what happened in between March 15 and July 31, of 1975? I had no other letters, no family informed me previously of any information previous to the month of my mother's passing, so I quickly called a family member for some clarification. I learned, yes, they had gotten back together after the March 15th letter and the plans were for her to quit her job on July 31, 1975 so the family could leave together and start fresh in another area... only for her to rush home and be left alone yet again with no clarification, answers or hope. I also learned during that call that she worked. She was a server at the diner within Howard Johnsons in

Darien, Connecticut. My mother and several aunties worked together.

I sit as a child of both my mother and father and will never question anyone's actions. I understand everyone has battles, a past, and deal with pain in different ways. I truly believe now is the time for doors to be opened, feelings to be dealt with and truth to be told. This will enable healing to surface as it has never been able to do in such a tough, dark, and tight past.

At the time of reviewing the documents given to me, I still had little information surrounding the day of my mother's murder until I continued to read more. Sitting very still, I read on the top of the next piece of paper:

"Certificate of Death" Patricia Ella Dickson, January 30, 1949 date of birth, Negro, age 26, August 13, 1975 date of death, Orchard St. Stamford Connecticut, Married, Spouse, a Housewife, Father listed was her step father's name and mother, my Grandmother, Lorrena McKelvy (Johnson), Hour of Death 2:50 pm on 8/13/75. The decedent was pronounced dead 8/13/75, hour 2:50pm. The incident was listed as a Homicide at a friend's home on Davenport Street Stamford Connecticut. Cause of Death... Stab wound to the left breast with penetration of left chest wall, left pleura and right ventricle wall, Hemopericardium medial stynum hemorrhage, left hemathorax, left thoracostomy with aspiration of blood., Certifier Name and State, date signed 8/15/75, Burial, Woodland Cemetery, Stamford Connecticut, 8/18/75, Bouton & Reynolds Inc. Funeral Home, Funeral Directors Name, Embalmers Name, Certification received for record on 8/18/75, Registrars Name, Certified Copy Stamped 11/6/75.

I breathe in and breathe out as the date and time registers. The explicit details flow in my mind as if I am getting stabbed while trying to get through the information. This translates to me as woman stabbed in the heart and bleed to death upon arrival to the hospital. Since I was a child, and still today, I ask over and over to myself, who would do such a thing and why?

As I whispered to myself what am I missing, while tears fell down my face, I realized my mother lived only a few more weeks after she wrote her last letter to herself. The words I translate into stating why? While seeing her cry out in despair, I ask myself if she knew her letter would be placed in my hands one day so closure and sense of it all would be revealed. The child in me wants to believe yes. The documents were not destroyed out of anger from her nor my grandmother who held onto them for 20 years before releasing them.

The dates Thursday July 31, 1975 through Wednesday August 13, 1975 (13 days, 303 hours and 50 minutes) is when I realize that my mother spent her last days alone with her children, maybe forcing a smile. She kept a face of faith and an "it will be alright" attitude. She kept her gentle demeanor intact, and held thoughts of what did I do, what did I not do, and what am I going to do deep inside! Even though I still wonder what crossed my mother's mind during each moment, second, hour and day, I will always keep the peaceful thoughts of it all in the forefront of my mind. Sadly, I feel closer to her than I have ever felt in my entire life. The more I research, talk to my auntie, look at letters and pictures, and still try to smile, I must believe that she had some peace at some time in her short 26 years of this thing called life. Even if only for a moment after the birth of her children resting in the hospital, looking down at her gifts who loved her as much as she showered love to everyone. I am grateful to feel a sense of her warmth and presence and an assurance that she would have been so proud that she did something right within her children.

So why did August 13th occur? Why would a woman whom I regrettably share the same name with have a (so called) friend of my mother, come to our home and tell my mother that another friend wanted to see her around the corner? Why would someone she trusted set her up with no warning? My mother who must have trusted the lady, we will call T, gathered myself and my siblings up. We all headed

43

around the corner only to find confrontation with the woman who wanted to assure she would have my father for herself and assure he would not return home to his family. This caused the moment to end with her murdering my mother. I do not remember the scene only a lot of noise, sirens from all areas arriving, my aunts screaming hysterically, and a lot of people all around. There was so much commotion. Who grabbed the kids? Where did we go? Did my mother look over towards us with fear? Did we get a sign to run? Did someone grab and shield us? Did we yell, cry, or even know what was happening? I will never know what my mother thought as the attack took place after trusting a friend walking around the corner as if it was a normal day.

- *You ever been doing something while gazing in the mirror and feel a lost presence or see the one you have lost within your face... This morning while in deep thought I know my Mother was ever so present, Lord I thank you for continual comfort when I may not understand myself or others around me. Thank you for reminding me of my mother's gentle and calm nature which helped her through her many battles...*

*#appreciatethosewhofillthespaces 5/25/2014*

Sadly, we must question, 'What a friend is? Who do we confide in and not.? Who do we trust fully?' At any given time, someone is always ready to stab you to get what they think should be theirs. I also learned the hard way in many instances as my kindness and giving the benefit of doubt caused me to miss the signs of many holding the knife while smiling in my face. Let's say lesson learned and I will stick with the few blessed friends I have from here on out.

## Chapter 4

What was my life to become as a six-year old with no mother? What was going on, where was she, was she coming home soon and why couldn't I remember her voice anymore? Thinking back, I can see her standing over my bed when I didn't feel good being very gentle in taking care of me. My siblings and I spent about two or three years with our grandmother after my mother's passing as she gained legal custody of us. This allowed us to go live with our father at a later date. Once he was settled and ready for us, my grandmother always stated she hesitated to release us, but always ended up doing what she thought would make us happy. Once she saw the joy on our faces when daddy came around, she couldn't resist.

Living with my grandmother and several aunts and uncles proved interesting as I sit back and think about it all now. We lived a very simple life with just what was needed. We had three people in one bed (the full-twin with iron pole headboards). I don't know how the boys slept as I didn't go into their room. We had a grandmother getting up early and cooking several different breakfasts to please different requests. School clothes pressed and laid on the bed and afterschool clothes awaited as we returned. She was, cracking peas on the porch, someone was scaling fish in the back yard, uncles and aunts were running in and out from who knows where, while some moved on. On occasion family gatherings consisted of music, cigarette smoke, playing cards and drinking at each other's houses while children ran in and out playing. I remember once, an uncle returned home with two beautiful dolls my sister's doll wore a red gown and mine pink as that was my favorite color. We sat them on the bed loving them as we always appreciated everything big or small given to us. Although at times, I would think to myself what else is life about. I can say many of those days were the good ole days as my mother's family loved us and always took care of Pat's kids.

I remember being introduced to a very small Baptist church which I learned my mother had sang in the choir. I do not know the name of the church although I remember it being near the village in Stamford, Connecticut next to a corner store. I am imagining hearing my mother sing in the choir as she held so much hurt within from her childhood through her short-lived young adult years. Did she cry while singing songs of praise as I do today? What was her relationship with the Lord like? Did she pray over her children and the unknown tomorrow? Or, did she simply believe what she endured throughout was how one is supposed to live. NO one truly knows what normal is in this thing called life.

My father would pick us up for some weekend visits, taking us swimming causing our aunts to be mad as they would have to redo our hair. It was a process to re-wash and braid, but they had to do what grandma instructed. And as I think back, I remember my father coming one Christmas and bringing loads of toys. One box my sister and I thought was a broom and mop set turned out to be acoustic guitars that we kind of frowned about because we wanted the brooms. Ha, Ha that was funny, but my father loving music always tied it into our lives somewhere. Ironically my birthday, Easter, and

Christmas throughout my entire childhood I can only remember great memories no matter what drama or tragedy was taking place at the time. Believe me some negative memories would surface such as a babysitter we use to go to. The timeline is foggy and I want to say it was when I was around 5 years old. If I am correct, she lived very close to our school. Sadly, I cannot remember anything nice about the lady who's name I cannot remember., I always wonder if she was a friend, family or just a lady who watched children. I know she was very strict and would force you to eat all the food on your plate if you liked it or not! Several times I recollect her serving canned ravioli to me, my sister and brother.

I would try to throw mine away or sneak to my siblings. Bless their hearts for trying to eat mine as well, but they would get caught and I was made to eat double. I still cannot fathom the thought of this food or even look at it without my mind going back to that exact time. She also had a lot of belts in sight although thankful to the Lord, she never hit us as she did other children.

- Resilient, how wonderful it is when a broken little girl could regroup and focus just enough within her little mind.

We stayed with our grandmother for some more time after that Christmas. During that time, I ended up having stages where I would blink my eyes uncontrollably. It turned out to be a bad habit and at times make weird movements with my mouth which annoyed my grandmother. I didn't know why my nerves began to act up or what I was thinking to cause it. I only knew I was a child and something wasn't right and missing in my life. I felt it within. During this time children were not taken to doctors and any acts a child did was brushed off and you were told "you better stop." I also would have the worst nightmares (until my young adult years and less frequent as I got older) which consisted of myself being in an empty room which looked identical to a room in my grandmother's home down the street from where we lived with my mother.

I would be in the room with a ball the size of a pea and in moments the ball would grow and continue to grow. As it grew my, breaths would get shorter and I find myself gasping for air until I would wake up fearful that I couldn't breathe. Who could I tell about this? What would people think? What would they call me? What was I to do? I got in trouble for squinting my eyes and moving my lips in a strange way and forced to stand in front of the mirror, so I could see how ridiculous (I was told) I looked. So, I wouldn't dare tell anyone I was having nightmares and couldn't breathe at times. Was I remembering the day of the murder? Was I making distractions to avoid remembrance? Was I experiencing so much trauma that I was slowly slipping away into a state of misunderstanding? This child did not know or understand. Again, I must believe that people did the best they could while dealing, or not, with their own circumstances at the time.

What was I to do with no outlet, no hope, and no understanding of death? What happened so fast, the change, feeling of loss while deep within, I was still waiting for my mommy to come home, as I felt everyone had stopped talking about her the way I wanted or needed. At that moment, I chose it was best to keep my thoughts and pain tucked within from this time and forever.

- Today I ask, are we paying attention to the children, the trauma, and triggers of it all? Do we question truly one's feelings while honestly waiting for an answer, embracing when crying or looking lost, and discuss the hurt and pain while explaining the situation entirely. For many, the answer would be no as too many still feel that children don't feel the effects of a crisis or understand as adults do. Children will snap back because they really don't carry the same hurt, etc. etc. etc.

I am amazed how the hurtful memories continue to surface. Although grateful, I still adore and carry my grandmother close to my heart. I'm blessed to have had her living with me during her last days. We had time to reminisce on the good times we had while I grew up and I shielded her from what was happening at our home after we left her. I cherish us cooking and shopping together and her spending countless hours talking with my son about the family, who was who and the happenings. At one point he stated to me how he knew more about the family then I did (I laughed within as I am sure at that time he did since I had suppressed it so far within).

## Chapter 5

The time had come for my father to retrieve us several years after my mothers' passing. When he did, we ended up in a blended household. He had remarried a woman who was always nice to me while she unknowingly taught me so much who had two sons of her own. Try to imagine how I must have felt during that time? It was a time that felt like the world stopped while I tried to keep the shattered pieces and thoughts of my mother attached in my head. There are still times I try to be quiet and think back to that time so long ago and pull a feeling or two from the past into today. I always wonder what that little girl was thinking. How did she feel about what was so unknown and foreign to her?

This was a new chapter in my short life which proved to be just as hurtful as the last. Although the lady who became my father's wife was very nice, I believe she tried the hardest she could, dealing or not, with her own shattered past. She was not the person, at that time, who could strengthen, mold, and help four little lost and confused souls. She tried and stuck it out in some form or fashion until the marriage dissolved sometime around 1987 physically, but emotionally, I believe was finished long before. We initially resided in her 3-bedroom apartment for I believe a year or a little less. Some dates mingle in my mind as trauma will cause you to have lapses in timelines especially if the period was traumatic. The place was very nice in a good neighborhood, with beautiful furniture. She had a good office job, the best clothing, and a nice car. This was very different from how we were accustomed to living with what was needed to survive. The accommodations I felt were odd with so many children now merged together. Her oldest continued to have his own bedroom while all the other children sleep in one room. I took note very early that her oldest son, who I believe was early high school age, was not in agreement with the current situation. Unlike us younger children, he could be vocal about how he felt and what he was not putting up with at the time. So, he kept his space, comfort, and peace. While I had to be in a room with my siblings and a stranger who did not think of the girls placed in his room as his little sisters. I thought it was odd how the rooms were arranged because all I could remember was sleeping with my aunties at my grandmother's home. Yes, it was cramped at times in the twin/full beds with the cast iron pole headboards, but the girls were always with the girls and my brother with my uncles unless he fell asleep with us from time to time.

I now understand fully why the son who was a couple year's younger than his brother didn't put up an argument and graciously welcomed the new change into his bedroom. Shortly after we moved in, he began to touch me while I slept. He always tried to enter the bathroom if I was in the shower. Back in those days there was only one bathroom in homes, so it was normal for a sibling to pop in use bathroom and run out laughing after they flushed the toilet making your shower cold. Not this step brother, he didn't do the normal annoying brother things because that is NOT how he saw the situation. To him, I was prey not a sister. I was someone who he thought would satisfy his need. Be medicine to his undiagnosed sickness. Oh, and let's not forget the numerous horrid car rides within the small white Pontiac car that we all had to squeeze into having to double up and sit on the older kids laps. He enjoyed this way too much. I know I was barely 10 not even in the double digits of age and wouldn't think is this normal. What is happening? Is anyone noticing what is happening, my confused face, any fear, was I beginning to act differently than how I previously acted? Do I bring it up in conversation with someone and if I do what do I say?! Will anyone believe me or will they be mad at ME? Sadly, the cars got smaller as we got bigger. It was on to a small four door blue Mercedes for my stepmother and my father's choice of car was a two-door black T-bird. How I must have smiled when finally, a black van pulled up one day for us allowing space for some freedom when having to pile in to go somewhere.

- Be careful blending families of any kind.

- Some boys do not look at your girls as their little sister.

- Evaluate all areas while knowing the background of the broken family you are placing your broken family within. (You all are broken for a reason.)

- Listen to your children's words and pay more attention to their actions and any drastic changes in their behavior, mood, weight gain/loss, characteristics, etc.

- Take note why they are seeking attention or not.

- Remind them who you are and be there for them in all capacities.

- Don't allow your daughters on anyone's laps and be so careful with your sons as well, abuse does not discriminate.

- Do not force children to hug or kiss anyone. I have always stated, children, senior citizens, and pets have the best instincts and are fast to pick up on someone's shady character or hurtful intensions. PAY ATTENTON!

As we transitioned into a four-bedroom house during the timeline of my

4th grade summer. I thought this has to be good. A lot will change. I was so happy that the girls will be in a girl's room and the boys in another. Yes of course, the stepmother's oldest son kept his own room until he graduated high school a few years later and moved out. He couldn't do that fast enough as this drastic change in his life I believe was never accepted. I always looked up to his strengths, drive, and self-assurance and I smile when I think of him and his achievements before he passed on. He never knew my admiration for him or how I yearned to learn to live free as he did with little or no remorse, finding and doing what we wished, no matter what. I keep a piece of him within, while I chose to have one of my sons carry his name. He may never know the impression he left or what was taught since he has passed on. I could only hope that sometime during our past he saw acceptance, approval and a piece of love shown through my own brokenness. I remind myself that he also didn't choose the cards we were dealt. Even though he was older, I am sure he had a lot of questions built up inside as well. We just dealt with them differently...

I remember some good times such as: holidays, family visiting here and there and us doing the same with them, baseball games with all the children in the family at the park (I was a good center fielder and pitcher), pool parties at an aunt and uncles house, my father sharing his passion for music with us, black culture, involving us in ballet, tap and dance and always going to the movies on Easter when it cost $1.00. We attended our stepmother's church St. John's Episcopal which was beautiful (It was very different from my mother's small Baptist church.). We sang in the choir and attended Sunday school every once in a while, and received our first communion there. I did enjoy Christmas Eve, Easter services and all the tradition in which it entailed. I remember Mr. Russel the organ player and having so much fun singing in the choir after running into church to get my black robe, placing the white topping over it, and lining up to march into church.

For some reason, I felt so much peace in this setting. That is where I enjoyed laughing without forcing a laugh to come out. I remember walking through the courtyards of the church and saying I think this is how life should be, clean, flowers blooming and the feeling of safety. I realize now that there was a God, that my Grace and Mercy who I profoundly state are my best friends now were oh so close to me when I didn't even realize it then. Signs were present, people and places where placed in my path to show me a little spark of light, a hint of hope, while spiritual hugs were embracing me when I felt at my loneliest.

- *"Now faith is confidence in what we hope for and assurance about what we do not see." Hebrews 11:1 (NIV)*

Too bad being in church was less than more. What I know now as abuse and not normal for step siblings (or any siblings) continued for several more years. He attempted to take the fondling to the next level as I slept with no regards to anyone in the room nor any fear of getting caught. I can't stress enough that people pull themselves together fully before introducing their children into brand new broken situations especially if they have already been through life altering events of any kind. I know life was so different back in the day and remarrying to have what the world calls complete households. It was thought a house ran better with a mother for small children and a man to be out at work and not worry too much about the internal happenings of the home. But my goodness, with that we still must be cautious in all areas. We must SEE what is happening and not just look at a situation. Take note of the hints thrown, or changes exhibited with a child all around. We must LISTEN and not just hear what we want when we want!

I remember sometimes going to church with my childhood friend "LaJune" as I call her. I am blessed to still be friends with her today after so many years. I would sit and listen to the music, the prayers, watch the interactions of families, how and what they did in church while telling myself they are so happy about something, even if I knew they had a bad day yesterday. I visited this friend recently and she made a statement as we talked about our past and the fun times we had playing jacks, baking hundreds of cookies during the holidays, and enjoying what children should enjoy no matter what was going on in our lives before or after. She referenced something like "You used to go to church with us (her family) when we were little" and the conversation carried on. I thought about that for several weeks later and said to myself, why didn't I go to that church more? I wanted to feel how they felt and how I felt when I was there. What I was feeling I can't explain and I didn't know what it was at the time. I just knew it was a safe feeling and at those moments I felt no one could hurt me or wanted too.

## Chapter 6

During that time in my life, I felt a sense of comfort and protection. Several years passed with me posting do not enter signs on my bedroom door. I started to eat more junk foods and crave sweets which was something that tasted good and unbeknownst to me at the time comforting. I didn't care what I looked like at that time while inviting weight gain. That could surely make me unattractive and keep that person away from me.

How ironic, for some reason our home was known as the place to be, 104 Moffitt St. Bridgeport, Connecticut. was where all the fun was happening. The parents were the coolest and we were so lucky to have it all...The saying what appears on the outside is not always as it is on the inside is very true in every facet. At the same time, people thought I lived an awesome life. During this time, as if I wasn't going through enough of the unknown, unexplainably I was introduced to people who could be cruel on the outside my house as well. Being bullied was introduced by a girl at a school we attended while our grade school was being remodeled. To see who you thought were your friends laugh with her was another push in the wrong direction in my mind. This has yet to fade or cease from within. Add this on top of what I was already enduring, how I was able to keep a right mind and not lose it at any given time, I truly believe I must have heard a quiet whisper or saw a glimpse of hope through some cracks within my life to make it this far.

Who wouldn't want to be at this house that was fun? There was something exciting always happening. Friends can come in and out. Family members (uncles) are welcome to reside within here and there, this year or that year. I don't think I can remember a time in my life when someone wasn't in need, dealing with a crisis, and needed someone's help. I remember hearing bits and pieces of both sides of the family tragic upbringings, who was dead, in jail, in trouble, in need... There were never positive conversations of triumph or anyone excelling (sadly we heard a few of these stories so much later in life.) Years later, I carried the look on my grandmother's face. It was a smile she wore so proudly as I walked down the graduation aisle. Did she know then that I was planning a future so different from what I had known?

Sometime before entering middle school, more change arrived. Something I always dreaded several paternal uncles flowed through the house. One lived with us longer than others and just long enough to add more misery to my already shattered world of confusion. He began to alternate evenings with my step brother and snuck into my bedroom to touch me in places an uncle shouldn't. He would pay attention to when I would go into the basement which housed the washer and dryer, their gym equipment, a drum set and my stepmother's extra clothing. I began to think there was no place in this house, in my life free, from what was happening. At times I would have nightmares of clouds getting bigger over me or being in a room with a small ball which grew and grew until there was no room for me and I couldn't breathe. This caused me to sleep in my father and stepmother's room on the floor at the end of their bed several times. Was the fear of someone entering my room getting to me, was I having what we know to be today anxiety attacks! Possibly, but who knew? Who asked, "how are you really feeling? Why are you starting to feel like this? What is wrong?"

Instead, it was, 'rest for today. I will bring some ginger ale and crackers home later.' This was the medicine of all medicines back when I was a child in my household. My uncle really thought it was okay to do what he was doing. He would afterward make sure I had some of his pocket change should I want to go to the store with my friends. In his sick mind, he assumed he was taking care of me. Or, what I understand now, he thought I was happy with a gift of money and wouldn't tell, I don't know! What do I tell? Who do I tell? With the current chaos and this one arguing with that one, who will I make mad? Will someone get hurt because of me? My goodness, I wish one of my vocabulary words in school at any time would have been "dysfunctional." What I couldn't understand at the time was that these people had many girlfriends so what was the need to bring me into the sickness of it all. At the time, I had yet to learn what was not normal, was not right, was in fact assault, abuse, hurtful, deceiving and wrong in so many ways. As several years passed, I started to feel free from this dark part of my life as people had moved out of the house. But was I free? I still made excuses for everyone's actions. Whether it was someone's age at the time, lack of common sense, lack of knowing, caring, or protecting (even if I felt they had to know.) I made excuses for many because of what I may have heard they went through in their own childhoods and relationships. Was it the way to think some may ask? In a mind of a child who yet knows her worth, this is the only way to think. I believe it is what kept a small portion of sanity together, strength to go another day and so much peace within.

- *"Those who are targeted, assaulted, hurting, have to know it is not you, it is not us, we are perfect in our own way, we are not broken, we are still glimmering as a spark of light is always within, we can continue to shine no matter what, we are glowing and someone is reaping the warmth of it even when we don't know it."*

I push to remember, relive, and write while I struggle through the pain of it all. While finishing what I have started over ten years ago, I'm repeating, this is the time! This helps me take the next step in this thing called life. Sadly, I find a lot of comfort in knowing that I will never go outside and accidently see, or one day at a family gathering, run into my stepbrother or uncle because they have both passed on. Sometime during the 1990's I received a card of apology that asked for forgiveness from my uncle. At that time, I thought I had forgiven him a little inside although I could never respond. I think and write about what they have done to me and for a period makes me want to vomit again and again as I start to choke on thoughts that are flowing about. While I try and suppress the hurt and pain that rises within and type each word, I remember the little girl who felt no one ever saw her except for the two people she hoped one day soon couldn't.

## Chapter 7

My eating disorder eventually grew from eating extra sweets to weight gain. So, to be unattractive and not be wanted grew to stages of bulimia which traveled with me way into my late 30's. Currently at times, I'm unable to eat large quantities of heavy food without my body telling me you know this is not staying down. A stomach ulcer was introduced to me during a school physical exam when I was in the eight-grade causing me to be aware of not getting too upset (stressed would be the word for today.) I tried so it would help eliminate any extra pain from occurring in my life. So now I have an issue that flares up when I'm upset. I'm sure the nurse who did the exam figured this young girl seems healthy and happy (which I portrayed perfectly) as she told me, "You will be fine." Over the years, I have mastered shutting my feelings off, being happy and content, and going with the motions no matter the situation at the time so the stomach pains would be less frequent and not hurt as bad.

Sometime in the transition of it all as a child I began to express myself with less assertiveness. In my mind, I was reminded my thoughts, cares and concerns would not be validated unless I was within my home. In most cases, I chose to not be a part of many conversations while just sitting and listening with, I am sure, a complacent look on my face. I thought why bother. What will change, or if it did, would it be any better or be worse? To me, change always meant I would hurt a little more than I did after the last change in my life occurred. I used to ask myself when growing up would my life had been different if I stayed with my grandmother? How would I have turned out? Would I have been a fuller or less the person I am today? Would I have had self-worth or dignity as a child had I not been molested by several weak people keeping strong within by myself. Today, I know who was holding me up and keeping me strong. Although as a child, if one person would have whispered don't worry you got this, we got this, you are going to do mighty things, you are so important and loved, then I would not have felt so alone, displaced, and so unsure for so many years to come. I did find comfort in visiting my grandmother after we moved back with my father. From this time on, she was living with someone who accepted us as his own grands, and she seemed happier and a little content. We would be placed on the bus and bother the driver with, "are we there yet?" as we visited frequently. The place was very nice and peaceful in the cutest neighborhood in Danbury, CT. I was always happy to be there because I felt so much security, normalcy, consistency, and structure, just how grandma's homes felt for many years.

I can still draw out the kitchen and other rooms in my mind smelling the place as if I just walked in it. I also cherish all my grown-up years with her and later being able to have her reside in Virginia with me. I will also cherish being able to spend her last days with her. The week before she left to be with my mother and brother she stated, "Karen, I have done all I will do, tasted all foods I can taste and have said all I can and need to say, so I know my time is near."

On Good Friday, April 6, 2007, I received a call from her. She was in a nursing home around the corner from my home. I heard, "Karen, Karen!" and then something about the nurses... One nurse got on the phone and stated, "We are getting her comfortable now." I thought nothing of it as the CHR center had always treated my grandmother like a queen.

I stated, "I will be over as soon as church is done within the next two hours" and we hung up. The next word I received about my grandmother was when my nephew found my twin sister (his mom), my husband and myself at a local church to inform us she had just passed. Wow was all I could say and I thought why I didn't go over to see her before church. I thought everyday about what she was trying to tell me when she called. The hurt of it all added to the pain I was already carrying through my life. How do I get away from all the

"What could I have done differently" in my entire life? I do find some comfort in the conversations we had prior to this day as I knew she was prepared to go. I graciously thank all the ladies of Antioch Baptist Church in Culpeper, VA who selflessly pulled themselves away from the service to comfort, console and assure us we were all right before we left to go see my grandmother. I smile today at the pure kindness shown.

No matter what happened in my life, I felt the need to keep a close connection with my grandmother and each moment I am grateful I did. That piece of relationship in my life proved tremendous for me overall as I longed to be close to and know a lady whom I struggle daily to remember...

My grandmother was the last piece of string holding me connected with some family members. With she and my mother now gone, I only cross paths with a few. I cannot allow so much dysfunction to cross back into my life or subject my immediate family to endure any of what I knew of. Knowing we all fall short at times and God is continually working with us, I do not judge. I simply know now how I have to choose to live and what God wants and promises me.

- *Make or become different.*

   *change, changed, changing*

Day to day, with each step taken, I learned that there was some strength within me. It had taken some time to locate it and years to understand where it came from. Telling myself as far back as I could remember something is not right, something is not right, something is not right. I knew this was not how I was supposed to be living. I would even state, if I didn't look like my family, I would have thought I was placed with the wrong group at birth. To keep focused, no matter what was happening to me, frequently I would pull myself out of the picture of my life. I would look inside to see where I was supposed to be, where shouldn't I be, learn who I was, try and remember something, anything, about my life before the woman I once called mommy faded away. So many days and years I slip back into another place. They slip so far within that I wonder how my life would have been if my mother had felt a bad vibe or a pain in her gut which caused her not to go around the corner on the one day that would change the future so drastically for so many.

## Chapter 8

Daily I wonder about my father and ask had he been dealt different cards during his life or turned the hand in for a redo, would the end of the game have been played differently. I continue to have questions logged in my mind from my inner child who patiently awaits answers, who understands the pain he and we all so tirelessly carry into each new year we are granted. Life is so short. Regardless if we live to 5 or 75 years of age, when we allow our mind to be taken over, our feelings to shut down and the past to win. I will always appreciate the 22-year-old young man who gave me life during a time when he was trying to find himself while dealing with his own past. As I continue, not knowing the depths of what and why so much pain had and continues to occur, I will always cherish about my daddy is that no matter what that is who he is. I can never list it all but will share some, I love being able to glance in a mirror and see my father's face then smile as I say, "I look just like my daddy." The intellect that traveled through him into me. Learning to play chess by him and playing many very long games as he strategizes like no other while explaining why every move had to be made. His ear for good music, the instruments we were introduced to, and him playing the song "Lovin' You" by Mini Riperton no matter how many times I said again! I appreciate the wonderful conversations we still have from time to time relating to world affairs and our people and so much more as I try to read between the lines to learn more of the past with hopes of one day having true conversations about our own family with no limitations. I smile as I remember him curling my hair for pictures to be taken by one of my uncles who loved photography. Wonderful Christmas with our traditional hot chocolate and new pajamas. I can't remember if this happened every year although, know it was more than less and something I in turn carried on to my own children. It's funny, as my boys got older, they loved and expected the pajamas, but not the hot chocolate so much. I remember telling them I am making this chocolate no matter if someone drinks it or not. I believe for me, I needed that one positive memory that traveled on for so many years in my memories to live on, so I could smile another day. I remember taking my last five dollars to buy cookie mix and carrots so my children wouldn't be disappointed about not leaving treats out on Christmas Eve. Well, they surely have outgrown that also, but at least, I find joy in my middle son continuing to want to bake all the cookies each holiday. It's so important to press positive memories in your children's minds.

I embrace the memory of my father teaching me to catch a soft ball while giving me his favorite baseball glove, then being so happy when the twins graduated High School and throwing the biggest party we ever had. This is a memory I keep near in my thoughts as it was something that finally tied my parents together. I will always cherish, once around 1996-97 when my father helped me move items into an apartment. Midway of carrying a piece of furniture he quickly paused as we laughed about something I said and my gesture and he told me I acted just like my mother and sounded just like her too when I said whatever I said. The disbelief on his face when he found out I loved Hershey bars as they were my mother's favorite. I always wondered about the day we moved the furniture did my dad have a flashback remembering of a time when he and my mother were moving something together and laughed about it? What gesture had I made allowing a door that was closed for so long to crack open with a response I had longed for and needed? A gentle hint of a woman the child in me once called mommy, was grateful to have that breeze of air in the form of knowing something about my mother. We continued to enjoy the moment. My heart felt warm and full a feeling I could never remember having before.

This also reminded me of someone telling me that my characteristics were so much like my mother's. We even slept the same and liked the same pajamas (I love the footies) also to the point of taking note that we both slept with a blanket covering up no matter how hot it was. I sit and think about that statement and think about it from my young girl's mind. I took a deep breath and sighed. I thought about a woman who I started to relate more to each day. I thought about the struggles we both fought through and did so well with a smile. In my mind, I concluded that a blanket was security, a barrier, our support... No matter how old we get or how far away from the pain of the past, we continue with a habit of comfort.

I continue at times feeling like the little girl from long ago who awaits questions to be answered relating to my father's family. His mother who on this day is still living, is an unknown relationship. It is unknown who she is, why the distance, and why were we kept away as children. I have one vague memory of seeing her in my entire life. It was while at a park when I was 9 or 10 years old and for a brief moment. What stories told to me or not should I believe? Feelings crushed to recently see on social media, a family member posted a picture of my stepmother taken from the late 70's or early 1980's. In the picture, she stood with my paternal grandmother and several other family members in my grandmother's kitchen. Where was I during this bonding period? To see a picture of a paternal grandfather and learn he passed later in life, I was shattered as well. To grow up thinking these two persons were deceased, who were never talked about, no information shared was heartbreaking. My paternal great grandmother who was also alive and not living too far from us as we grew up was heartbreaking as well. I did receive a crystal dish of hers after her passing which is all I have to hold onto. People also said, "she was the sweetest person." How come such a nice person wasn't allowed to be a spark of light within my dark world I still ask? I do compare my great grandmother's pictures to mine and like to say I have her shoulders. I compare my wedding picture to a picture of hers. I wonder do I get my poise and ladylike ways from her? What did she sound like? I think up stories while looking at her beauty in the very few pictures I have.

- *"We all have to do better when children are involved, when they are young adults and at a certain point in their lives, give them the resources and space to make decisions and choices for themselves regarding family. Allow them to evaluate what's best for them, for when we don't, we have so many broken minds being*

104

*filled with so much of the unknown on top of the hurt that seems to never stop."*

- *"Times will get tough although in many situations your children don't need to know every issue you as a parent are battling with. There is truly a time and place for every conversation. Think about how stressed you may get worrying about grown up issues and then times that by ten for your child. They cannot carry a load that we know is too heavy for us to carry from time to time."*

- *"I can no longer find fault from my past nor figure out the unknown as that is hard to do when others have a story of their own way down inside. We must build ourselves up, keep our mind active, read, and talk when feelings are down. Stop with the wonders and whys while breaking cycles. Close windows that keep allowing destruction and chaos in our lives. Hard to do yes! But why not work towards it each day. Remind yourself just how strong you are."*

- *"Give your worries to the Lord and not people. Many are ready to share your testimony (to make themselves look better) when you may not be, causing more hurt, pain and distrust."*

Jesus said He would carry our burdens and as hard as it is, we have to start giving them to Him. Stop placing them on and within our children's lives. Matthew 8:17 reads: *He takes on all our suffering.* Today I can believe this to be true.

Although many thoughts and questions may continue to linger in my mind, periodically, I continue to piece this thing I call life together, the little girl in me can breathe a little lighter. Her heart stops fluttering so quickly within her chest as she courageously whispers, I made it through yesterday.

So, what happened to the child

who was forced to grow up

wrapped in many layers

of hurt and pain?

Did comfort

or love

come easy

and with no cost

or did the doors to more

hurt and pain open up once again?


I'm so glad you asked...

# ABOUT THE AUTHOR

A child of the Almighty God, Karen D. Brown has devoted her life to being compassionate and caring while spreading the Gospel and Love of Jesus Christ. Karen is a native of Stamford Connecticut, the child of Mr. Coleridge J. Dickson and the late Patricia E. Dickson. Mrs. Brown Shared her parents with two sisters and one brother and later in life blessed with 3 younger siblings.

Mrs. Brown a former school teacher in Connecticut continues to hold a special place within her heart for all children. Serving as a lifetime advocate for abandoned, misplaced children and young adults has been very fulfilling. She has found joy in assisting pregnant girls who are alone, displaced, giving support during labor & delivery, but most of all unconditional love and a lot of hugs. The numerous persons who have crossed Mrs. Brown's path allowing her to mentor, assist with housing needs and teach basic home and life skills has in return blessed her tremendously.

Mrs. Brown has worked in the mental health field for almost 20 years, and the previous Director within a Sexual Assault and Domestic Violence Agency. Mrs. Brown continues to assist many in need relating too domestic violence, sexual assault, and a host of other circumstances, while thriving daily with the Lords assistance to reach and touch those who have yet to find their voice as they silently cry out for help.

Mrs. Brown along with her husband have co-founded Mentoring Moments. A mentoring program in which they provide counseling, support, and love with the Lords guidance.

Mrs. Brown has served within the Ministers Wives & Ministers Widows Association of the Wayland

Blue Ridge Baptist Association; Virginia Chapter, providing love and support to those in need, volunteering and donating within the communities while uplifting one another within the ministry. Mrs. Brown is the First Lady of Pilgrim Baptist Church, Locust Grove VA; she adores her church family who has graciously and wholeheartedly accepted her into their hearts. She enjoys singing in the choir, serving as a deaconess, teaching Sunday school, and working within the women's ministry. She is married to the humble Pastor Garry M. Brown, mother of three sons and Nona to four beautiful granddaughters. Loving the Lord from deep within Mrs. Brown lives daily by the Word, her favorite book in the bible is Proverbs as she strives for wisdom each day